EMERGENCY BRAKE

Ruth Madievsky

TAVERN BOOKS

PORTLAND

Ruth Madievsky, 1991-

ISBN-13: 978-1-935635-53-6 (paperback)
ISBN-13: 978-1-935635-54-3 (hardcover)

LCCN: 2015960179

FIRST EDITION

9876543 Second Printing

TAVERN BOOKS
Union Station
800 NW 6th Avenue #255
Portland, Oregon 97209
www.tavernbooks.org

I

II

For my grandparents,
Yefim Galper and Roza Kordonsky,
and in memory of my grandmother,
Anna Galper

JANUARY

When January lifted its head
to a slow applause,
the hinges of everything alive
opened like fruit.
I felt you and I could fit
in the mouth of a spoon,
like we were coconut extract
or a bump of cocaine,
pollen and benzodiazepines
and the sound of wind
making love to a clothesline,
I thought maybe we were made
of the same photons as light,
I thought about how I had never
made a dent in anything
using just my skull,
and then January unpeeled inside me
like a nicotine patch,
and then I let myself get stuck
in the alley between my lungs.
I let my body
become a bedtime story
with knights and horses
and a fire-breathing dragon,

and then I made you dress up
as the fire-breathing dragon
and, like everything else,
that felt good until it didn't,
like downing more cocktails
than the number of letters
in my name.
Yes, I bought the poet a drink,
but I wasn't trying to fuck him,
yes, I swallowed a beehive
and tasted my fist.
Eugene died.
We gave him to the fire.
My tongue wore a lab coat
and yours turned into menthol,
I pricked the fingers
of many strangers,
took a head count of their blood.
I guess mostly I think
about how people
turn back into objects
and how we don't know
what to do with those objects,
so in the end
we pay someone
to put them somewhere else.

SHADOWBOXING

To let grief ride my blood.
To say *eye* but mean *staircase*.
To wonder how many times
the suitcase inside me can open and shut.
What it would take to shatter
a wine glass in my hand.
To want desperately to be queen of something.
Queen of crying in coatrooms, queen of waiting
for the medicine to take.
To let the rabid dog of anxiety off its leash.
To wear the brass knuckles of loneliness.
What was it between us that went out?
Why do I feel like an x-ray patient all the time?
To address someone I love
the way a knife is thrown at a tree.
To let my brain swallow the mouthwash.
To ask the usual questions, whose fingernail, whose condom.
If I throw enough lamps, will you come.

HOTEL

Whenever I wonder whether our bodies
are more like paper or scissors,
whenever I feel like a long knock
on a slab of wood that hasn't decided yet
whether it wants to be a wall or a door,
I think about the hotel we stayed at
where I turned into bubble-wrap,
how night opened us,
the envelopes we are.
I have never claimed to be an oxygen mask
or the kind of person who understands
the difference between a tongue
and a tackle box, but I know
that there is ceremony
in the sound of a body
becoming a lit match.
When the music in the room above us
turns out to be the ceiling fan,
I think of all the bathtubs we've entered
the way flags enter planets,
how we've been Windex-ed out
of each hotel room's history.
I am the square of chocolate
on the pillow, sometimes the hand towel

forced into the shape of a swan.
Mostly I wish empathy
took shorter cigarette breaks,
that I understood the need
to walk the corridors
of another person's flesh.

HALLOWEEN

When my boss tells me my love of Halloween
is indicative of a love of kinky sex,
I take another sip of the dark beer
I've been nursing—which tastes
the way ashtrays smell
but is comforting to hold, the way it's comforting
to grip a flashlight when you are camping
and wake in the middle of the night needing to pee
but not wanting to do so on a member
of a different species—my fingers wrapped
around the beer's neck, a collar on a dog,
and what I wouldn't give at this moment
to be a dog, asleep by a fireplace
or even chained in a yard, miles
from this man who is eyeing my empty shot glass
as though looking up a skirt,
our coworkers laughing, throwing back Jim Beam,
while I hover above the bar
thinking of all the women I know
who would sleep with him, women who mean something
different than me when they use the phrase
rubbed the wrong way, and how all my life
I've been about as carefree as a soft peach
in a pile of broken glass, my hand

always twitching toward the Ativan bottle, always ready
to pull the emergency brake, this fantasy
I keep having of being sucked into an MRI machine
like a film being rewound, skipping past
the good parts—kissing in Ferris wheels,
feeding each other pasta—landing instead at the part
where I'm a truck that won't start, where I leap
down the elevator shaft of night.
Now my boss is ordering another round
for us all, his insides a few drinks shy
of becoming his outsides, and outside
is a world of minimarts and hypodermic needles
where I will one day have to answer
for the things I said
when I was feeling like unclaimed baggage,
for making loneliness into a kind of fetish,
letting it tie me up, and telling it to beat me, to do it now
and do it hard, to empty me out
like a stomach, like a pocket
swollen with coins, to fuck me
the way a shovel fucks the earth, so I can stop
thinking about IV chemo and mausoleums,
so I can pretend not to hear my brain
trying to eat its way out.

ATROPINE

I took my first birth control pill
the night my neighbor slammed his girlfriend's
head into the fridge.
I was reading about atropine,
how it tells the heart
to pedal faster,
how it sucks the spit right out of your gums.
Police came, kicked in the door,
found my neighbor with scratches across his face,
standing among the shards
of the smashed television set
the way a dog will stand
in its own mess.
I think of them when I hear car brakes
or squeeze a plum so tight
the meat spills out.
They didn't get evicted.
She didn't throw her
combat boots and Joan Didion novels
into a suitcase, fly back to Indiana
to wait tables at her cousin's seafood restaurant.
As far as I know, they're still together,
still overcooking chicken and throwing firewood
in their chimney's mouth,

their walls still empty,
still the white of scars.
That's how it is sometimes:
one person gets to be the can of 7-Up
and the other has to be the finger
floating inside.

IF THE BODY IS A DOOR

I remember wondering whether the body
             was a pool, if it could be entered that easily,
     the way I enter dreams and play every character,
             one version of me petting the dog
                     while another sets the schoolchildren on fire,
and how the body is fire, this choice I have never had
             over what makes it burn.
                     I remember when your mouth
         was a city I entered dancing.
             I remember being nine
                     the time a stranger stuck his hand down my shorts.
His penis rose like a fever,
         something inside him trying to torch its way out.
                 This is another way of saying
     that the body is a form of restraint,
             and that restraint, like blood, deserts the body quickly.
     When I remember the past as burglary,
I think the body is a door, and what is a door
                     but a crime scene waiting to happen,
     the way a needle waits to happen to a vein.
             No matter how many times I mistake television light
for the moon,
                     someone will always walk through my neighborhood
         carrying their body blade side up.

The waffle house will pretend
no one was opened like a tangerine in its parking lot.
The human heart will remain
the size of two fists.

TINY SHOTGUN

There is a tiny shotgun
behind both eyes.
If not my eyes, my lungs.
If not my lungs, an ambulance must be going by,
its siren a hole I climb into,
wondering about the person inside
and whether he is coming or going,
whether she will be making any more egg white omelets.
I've been thinking about disinfectants in urinals
and how they're called cakes,
which is similar to the time I told Alice
her boyfriend was a gentleman
for driving me home
and left out the part
where he put his hand on my ass
and also the part where I didn't tell him to stop.
There is something about cheap wine and leather jackets
I want nothing to do with.
Let's play a game:
you get to be anything you want
and I get to be something that's not antifreeze.
Let me be a slow dance
or a dime in a fountain, something
that won't leave you in a stairwell

like a spit-laced cigarette,
something more than the air in a fist.
I don't know why my hands
keep turning into asthma inhalers,
why lately everything has been storm clouds
and operating tables. I have locked myself
in the pantry with three matches
and a bag of ice. I guess this is winter,
the breakfast, lunch and dinner of it,
I guess I feel like an earring
in a hotel parking lot,
a blacked-out window
in a community theatre
where, inside, one woman is telling another
the difference between pain
and the idea of pain, and the man selling tickets
is sucking on a jawbreaker
and trying not to think
about crash sites and government cheese.

CACTUS

I'm sitting beside a cactus in a stranger's backyard,
trying to remember the last time
I celebrated something that wasn't a holiday.
I'd like to call last night a celebration,
how the sheets drew around us like a prom dress,
how my fingers were out partying all night
in the disco of your mouth. Anyone who says
they don't want to be celebrated
is lying. We all want champagne corks
praising each slip knot
of the tongue, each the launch code
for another bottle rocket to fire,
streaking across the sky
the way a peeled dress slices the dark.
I'm stroking the cactus between its quills,
wondering when was the last time
the man whose house I am renting was celebrated,
when someone last took him
in her mouth. Years from now,
when we've walked out of all our photos,
we will remember the doves we coaxed
from each other's throats,
blood and sunlight, the neck an altar,
how we took each other like barbiturates.

SOME MORE THINGS I DON'T KNOW

I don't know if Leo is in jail,
and I don't know who to ask.
I have this vague memory
of there being a trial,
of Vera coming to school late one day,
not wearing her uniform.
I don't know his last name
or why I keep trying to find him
on Megan's List, why I keep scrolling
through the one hundred and sixty eight pages
for Los Angeles County,
over three thousand
Lewd Or Lascivious Acts
With A Child Under 14 Years Of Age,
if he even lives in LA County,
if he's married or single,
dead or alive,
if I'd recognize him without the hat.
That day at school was the first time
I saw a girl my age wearing a blazer.
I wanted to cry because it made her look older
than ten, which couldn't have been the point.

BOBSLED

I want my name to amount to more
than a bone passed between two dogs. I don't
want catheters or shrink wrap or any more ceremonies
of fists. I want each rib in my body
to hold the shadow
of a lion. I don't want strychnine. I don't want
to be the rind on the orange.
Let's make Ouija into a drinking game,
play strip Trust Fall. Let's not be knockout
pills. I'd like to pass a cherry seed
back and forth with our tongues,
but I don't want the panic attack after. I'll keep
the three orgasms. I'll keep the night
we were thunder gods, the night I learned
the moon has no light of its own,
I'll keep unbuttoning my shirt
one button too many, I'll keep the feeling
of being on two planets at once
but mostly on the one where you are
melting butter in a pan, where popcorn
is popping and there is rosé wine on the table, which
is the same planet on which, in sixth grade,
Marcus told me he prefers shoe shopping
to football, and I told him,

That's exactly why everyone assumes you're gay.
I don't want the electrons that left his face
and landed in my backpack. I don't want meanness
to bobsled the icy bank of my thoughts.
When I open, I want to be the umbrella,
not the pocketknife.

SHADOWBOXING

Here are the sex cries
my neighbors threw against my walls,
here is the hair you left on my pillow,
here is the sound I made when I found out
my grandfather has cancer,
here are the bats
that sleep in my lungs.

Here is the fire escape
and here is what happened on the fire escape,
a matchbox, a light bulb,
a box of Sudafed, scissors.

Here is my body making love to its shadow,
music of teeth against teeth,
lips against neck,
my body a basketball hoop,
a flat tennis ball, broken beer bottle,
here is the prescription
I haven't worked up the nerve to fill.

Here is Los Angeles
begging someone to hold its hair back while it vomits
a gas mask, a lighter, a butterfly
with its back wings torn off.

Here is a concave mirror.
Here is me falling into the concave mirror.
Here is the question
of where I will land or if.

BOX OF SHADOWS

I want you to imagine a box.
Inside the box, the shadow of the hospital

where you were sloughed from your mother
like a grape. And before that,

before skin and seed—
the shadow of your father's first kiss,

of mornings he woke
feeling like a tooth in the devil's gums.

He strolls through your face
like a park he has known since he was old enough

to forget the difference between praying
and thinking about space.

Think about space. Imagine the shadow
of the planet whose atmosphere

is the color of what you hate most
about yourself, whose rings are the hips

of the woman you picture when you are asked
to picture death. What does she keep

in her pocket? What is the taste
of your name in her mouth?

II

NIGHT

is a story the hypothalamus tells itself

Once, I was the hole
in the wall I was punching

Night carries a scalpel

Once, a man asked for my mouth
like he was asking to bum a cigarette

Night is an exit wound

Once, there was nothing more dynamite
than a fast car and a hand up a dress

Night is a bra clasp

Once, I dreamt of the space between your thighs
and woke with a lit match on my tongue

Night is a mouth

Once, everything I wanted to know
came down to sex or suffering

Night is a mouth becoming a door

FALLING ACTION

Tonight my name is the pearl onion
I place on your tongue,
the sound a pelvis makes
when it opens.
Tonight the fly beating its head
against the ceiling light is drunk
from the wine
we opened and forgot about.
You turn me over,
a poker card.
You turn me over
like the list of side effects
I explained this morning
to the woman
dying of colon cancer.
I'm touching all twenty-seven
bones in your hand,
wanting to hang a sock
over the door
of what I can't stop thinking—
that it's cold inside the body,
even inside a burning body,
and all that we love
becomes the atoms

of something else.
Tonight I'm looking at a man
but seeing a handprint on a window.
Something inside me
scattering like deer.

SHADOWBOXING

I'm trying to re-wire the bomb
of my body.
It must be spring.
I must be telling you
about the time I stayed up until four in the morning
to catch the end
of my friend fucking a stranger.
How I saw it as less of a violation
because he didn't love her.
I can't tell the difference anymore
between myth and medicine.
I remember how happy he looked the next morning
better than I remember
my high school graduation.
The radiator coughing up its heat.

POEM FOR SPRING

Mid-March in Los Angeles
and the cats are in heat,
purring harps
that ache to be stroked the right way,
and I'm thinking about gauze
in the neighborhood deli
as we swap bites of macaroni
and spoonfuls of cabbage soup,
and there's a charge
on every doorknob
and also between us
and someone has died
but I don't want to talk
about that here,
and one of us has a cold
and will give it to the other
by accident,
inasmuch as two people
throwing each other around
on a towel in the backyard
is an accident,
and the body is a pillbox
and God's apology is orgasm
and the button on your jeans

is as old as the universe,
which is to say,
sing your aria, little man.
I want every cat on this block
to get some
and for every person to forget
the waiting rooms and surgical lights
of winter, the harsh soap
and the cruelty of moths.
Spring is upon us,
and the only violence
we have time for
is the violence of stars.
So kiss me
on the sauce-spattered table,
let the pasta stick to the walls.
Make me forget
that I am both the box
and the box-cutter,
the sutures and the banana.
Your collarbone is a balcony—
let my lips be the birds.

TUNING FORK

I was telling strangers at the birthday party
about all the ways in which our cells
are trying not to be forest fires.
How inside each cell
is a tuning fork
and inside each tuning fork,
the coiled music of our DNA.
I was floating somewhere between
the beer cooler and the red eyes
of three cigarettes
the way I imagine silk floats
inside a spider.
Inside, my friend was calling his mother
in the bathroom,
while outside,
the woman he wanted to love
picked a hole in her tights.
I was close enough to catch
the blue smoke that escaped her,
which was closer than the distance
between the benzodiazepine in my pocket
and the back of my throat.
I am always running toward
or away from myself.

We picked at a cake
someone bought at a supermarket,
toasted to mercy
though none of us knew
what it meant.
I guess I am asking
why the mind has a shorter memory
than the body.
Whether the language of the body
could ever fit inside a throat.
My friend told me he wished
for someone to treat his body
like a public park.
I'm sick of careful, he said,
which got me thinking about why
some days I am
a narrowly avoided bike accident,
and on others
I have been tree-ringed
by the man who took my silence
to mean yes.

PROPOFOL

My kidneys are leaning into the wall of my back
like a pair of boxing gloves,
the way my grandfather is leaning
into the idea of an operating table,
a paralytic agent, his body
a space station for someone else's hands.
I work in the hospital where it will happen.
I work and wait for the part
where the lungs I keep wanting this month to be
stop huffing propane, stop threatening
to make like my patient's vein
and collapse. Inside
the sterile compounding room,
I shoot drugs
down an IV bag's gut. I listen
to the outer-space hum of machines
that eat the air out of the room.
There is nothing sexy
about incision.
There is nothing about the phrase
nasogastric tube
that makes me want to look
both ways before crossing the street.
I want to hold him

like he is something other
than a mucus membrane.
Like maybe the planet inside him is Pluto,
like it's not really a planet at all.

ONE SPRING

I kept breastfeeding
my existential anxiety

One spring

I had an empty stomach
for a face

I had a boyfriend

One spring

I kept telling the same story

I kept telling the same story
so I wouldn't have to tell
the same story again

One spring

I was the smoky remnants
of a campfire

One spring

I watched a dragonfly circle my pool
for two hours and felt happy

I felt happy
and like a blueberry
in the mouth of someone who loved me

I felt like the squeak a stair makes
under a bare foot

One spring

I heard the pills inside me
go quiet

I heard the washing machine
trying to beat the blood out of my dress

One spring

I thought a lot
about photosynthesis

I thought a lot about stem cells
and whether they were conspiring against me

I thought about war

and how armor outlives the people
it's there to protect

One spring

I wondered if anything is really here
to do anything

One spring

I felt one
with the doorstops at Home Depot

I found myself inside a salt shaker,
inside the smell of super glue

I found a photo of the girl I never was
and always will be

I pulled the apple
from her mouth

MOUNTAIN

July is giving me
the kind of look
that makes me think
it might throw something,
might lift me up
and leave me on a mountain
where the air is thin
as a thirty-gauge needle
and makes my head
feel like a balloon
a kid is stuffing rocks into,
and I have nothing
new to say about helping my brother
into an x-ray gown,
slipping the booties
over his socks
and telling the joke
about how an anesthesiologist's
wife might not realize
she's being abused.
Lately it feels like every joke
I tell was less offensive
in the original Russian,
like every poem I write
is an act of public indecency.

I know I've gotten good
at being everywhere
and nowhere at once,
at constructing gods
and invoking them
the way a waitress might invoke
a Caesar salad.
My mind holds a brick
until it becomes the brick,
and I am constantly forgetting
that my body owns me,
not the other way around.
I spend most days hoping for release
and not knowing from what.
I don't know what scares me more—
the white noise inside the body
or the quiet.
I drive home with my brother
and a printout of his bones.
How strange
to hold a picture
of what he looks like
from the inside:
the curve of his spine lit
like a silent film star.

SHADOWBOXING

I was waiting for my hairpins
to turn back into gods,
I was waiting for my pillow
to stop resembling a guillotine,
I was wondering whether I was
the burnt rubber on the highway,
the wad of gum
my brother swallowed
and the stomachache that followed,
I was feeling like both the scalpel
and the kidney,
like I had opened a back entrance
into a classroom
but the classroom had left,
like I was carrying my dead
in my back pocket,
which was also full of bees,
like the blood inside the bees
and the hemoglobin
inside the blood,
like everything
I had ever told my lover
was tap-dancing down my spine,
I kept seeing myself

wrapped around him
like a car around a tree,
I let the slow insomnia
of August
build a condo in my head,
tear the plastic off the furniture
the way I sometimes
tear off my dress,
I fed myself to a screen door,
I let my mouth
become a matchbook,
I lit myself on fire,
I didn't light myself on fire,
but something smelled like it was burning,
some piano inside me
fell over, my left hand
gave my right hand sleeping pills,
and my right hand took them.

SIDEWALK

You are probably alive
somewhere in the world,
and I don't know how I feel
about that. You're tightening
the screws of a run-down swing set
in an apartment complex in Hollywood
and winking at the girls
who are waiting on the grass for you
to finish: girls with Lisa Frank notebooks
in their backpacks and macaroni and cheese
in their teeth, girls who
don't have breasts yet,
girls with mothers
who fishtailed their hair
before school that morning and fathers
who won't let them see
PG-13 films. Or maybe
you're eating a peanut butter sandwich
in a prison cell, peeling the crust
like a bitter store clerk
tearing the dress off a mannequin.
You're buying extra-small
thongs at Victoria's Secret. You're sinking
your nails into the skin of a peach.

You're licking your fingers. I think
I need to stop thinking. I think this sidewalk
is made of the same material as tombstones.
I think that if you ever
met the moon, you would
grab her by the throat.

NESTING DOLLS

I've been waking with an empty net in my hands.
　　　　　I've been re-reading the Neruda poem
　　　about the rain taking off her clothes.
　　　　　　　　Tonight the moon is a surgical mask,
　　　　　the stars psych ward refugees.
Somewhere in this zip code,
　　　　　　　　　two teenagers are making a backseat holy,
　　　their hips harmonizing the radio,
　　　　　　　a gun in the glove compartment.
　　　There is always a gun
　　　　　in the glove compartment,
　　just as there will always be parties
　　　　where I accept a ride home
　　　　　　　from someone whose name
　　　　　I've spent the last two hours
　　dragging through dirt.
　　　　　　　　Right now, you think I'm eating pasta
　　with a friend who has a PhD
　　　　and a dog and doesn't feel like a spare tire
　　　　　　most of the time.
Really, I'm home,
　　　thinking about nesting dolls
　　and how all my life
　　　　I've been a charley horse in the thigh of some god.

There's this dream
where my heart is a salted pretzel,
which is better than the one where my body is a looted ship
which isn't a dream at all.
I keep thinking we are in the temple
of the apathetic ghost
or picturing us on Plymouth Rock,
where I am burying the flag of my finger
beneath the band of your jeans.
Call me an armchair romantic.
Call me when you finish your Old Cuban,
when you leave the bar
with the beautiful women on tap,
so I can tell you
I've decided not to be a broken window anymore.
It's going to be all rapid-fire dick jokes
and YouTube videos of Celtic dance
from here on out.
We'll be a Labor Day barbeque.
I'll be the watermelon
and you can be the spoon.

BRIDGE, SHADOW, HAND

I want to say something about bridges,
      bridges and hands, how when you hold hands on a bridge
   it no longer feels like a bridge,
          how after, watching a lit candle do that thing you like
with the dark, you decide it doesn't matter
     whether your life is simple in its collapsibility
   or collapsible in its simplicity,
        you think the questions you have with yourself
            are tinted vials in a medicine cabinet,
     who cares if your body
       is a dormant volcano,
  what does it matter which of your friends have picked out names
      for their first three children
             while you spent most of the day
          feeling like a receipt someone forgot at McDonald's,
and can I just share this theory
    that a person can fall down her own shadow,
      that sex is not always about breaking and entering
   though both involve thresholds and hands
and sometimes cuffs for those hands,
         what is it anyway about hearing someone you love
  speak your name
      that's like being rocked back and forth,
is there anything more sacred

than that person's mouth,
how it opens like a renaissance,
how it is always a metaphor for sex,
so you are an astronaut
each time you necromance another curve of the body,
so you have this desire
to touch other people's things,
it's all relative, the way you enter the museum of love,
how you are always standing too close to the paintings,
leaving the blue of your breath
behind as a fingerprint,
it's okay, it's alright, this bridge isn't going anywhere,
the maple leaves are happy to see you,
the water below doesn't want you in its arms,
you are not going to fade out like a cough,
the person whose skin you are touching
wants you to read it like braille,
this blood rollercoastering your arteries
says, *Put his finger in your mouth,*
think about the merging of shadows,
imagine the body as a lamp,
which it is.

THE SPACE BETWEEN

In the opening and closing
of moonroofs on the freeway,
in the space between two objects, two people
who aren't touching,
in the differences between your lover
and a childproof cap,
your body and a torn guitar string,
synapse and reflex, scalpel
and condom. The dry cough
and the wet cough.
Night and its carnage.
I used to wait for someone
to tug on the rope inside me.
I used to think I was held together
by the same things that hold a poem
together. There's the distance
separating my hand and the cab it's hailing,
the hail and the windshield,
the shield of nervous laughter
while talking to strange men
and the genuine fear like a stove
I keep leaving on.
Minor key and major key.
Sex and sex crimes.

Faith being the belief that there is a distance
between yourself and your self.
Despite what anyone tells you,
two people can touch without touching.
A person can unravel
like the thread that ties clouds together,
and sometimes all anyone can say about it is,
Wasn't it weird when she turned into vapor
like that?
There's a limit to how much the blood
can absorb, convert to batteries,
there's only so much
a person can take.
Eventually we all end up ambulance sirens,
the distance between the drive to the hospital
and the hands in our chests.
When you live in a city of struck matches,
you start to notice how space
dilates and constricts like a pupil.
You start to wonder how many more times
you will ride cruelty's handlebars
and if that's fewer than the number
of times you will drive to work
as the hollow bones of a bird.
I want to tell you about the arcade
and the cough syrup,
how there's a difference between loving someone

and letting someone you love obliterate herself
though I'm not sure what that difference is.
On the radio, someone is singing
about the doorway-ness of eyes
in a way that makes me think
they've never actually seen eyes.
In the dream, his penis
is shaped like an arrowhead
and I don't know what to do with that
any more than I know what to do
with this image I have
of myself chained to a hospital bed,
a nurse walking toward me
with a loaded syringe.
I've become obsessed
with the naming of things.
The distance between a word
and what it signifies—
is it larger or smaller than the distance between
the scream and the throat muscle
that creates the scream?
I'd like to float on the raft
of pills between your ears.
I'd like just once for my belief in my own sanity
to clear the front yard, the yard over,
the hill where we played soccer
when I was a person who played soccer,

the gas station where I realized
there is almost no space
between a wound and the story
behind or in front of it,
the gas station where we started lying to each other
and I'm not sure we've ever stopped
or that we should.
I could have been a machine
with gumballs inside it.
I could have been the sleep inside an infant
or that thing that disappears from the room
when your girlfriend tells you
what a middle-aged man did to her
the summer she was nine.
Maybe I can still be something like
the lens of a camera,
the space between what you see
and what you get.

LIGHT SWITCH

My lungs are afraid of the dark.
I can hear them now,

locking the door of my ribcage
now that this light in my chest

has become the memory of light,
now that I'm floating

above the harbor of my body,
have left my shadow to steer the ship,

which I tend to do
when asked a question like,

Are you sure you didn't imagine it?
You were very young.

My hands remember every forest
they've wandered into.

Inside me is a pack of Mentos
I am feeding to a Coke bottle,

the sound of a penny thrown in a blender,
shuddering that has nothing to do

with bodily danger and everything to do
with being spoken to like a stopped clock.

My lungs keep trying to be fire escapes.
My lungs are the piano strings

of everything I'm not saying
wrapping their chords around my neck.

I use my body as flint.
If suffering is the cousin of lust,

then this bridge I am building
out of condom wrappers and caution tape

is how I scale the wall of insomnia,
another throat I'll have to cut.

EVERYONE I LOVE IS DRAFTING THEIR OWN EULOGIES

in parking lots, in bedrooms,
in supermarkets between the ground beef
and the egg noodles. Let's try that again:
so much comes down to a body
handcuffing itself to its ghost.
I want to tell you about the time
the past was an earring
under the bed. How I lived
in the space between touching
and not touching, how I wanted
everyone I love
to wear me like a hat. Now I'm the darkness
a city bus moves through,
but not always, not when I pass someone
walking more than three dogs,
not when everyone I love
is working full-time as my lungs.
In Los Angeles, someone's replaced
all the oxygen with surgical grade stainless steel,
someone's tagged all the freeway overpasses
and I can't tell if they wrote *HELEN*
or *HELP*. Everyone I love is trying
to shine me like a flashlight,

everyone I love is telling me
to say ahh. In my backyard, forty ants
are sharing a slice of watermelon,
and I don't know why that makes me feel
lonely, why I wish I was their size
and with them, fighting for the juiciest piece
with everyone I love
or just letting them have it.

BECAUSE IT'S OCTOBER

and I'm watching ambulance lights
bathe a motel
and not thinking
about the loose glitter
my mouth is,
because everything inside me
isn't rattling
like a change purse,
not splitting
into smaller versions
of itself,
small enough to be threaded
through the eye of a needle,
I think my brain
is done swallowing itself
the way the ocean
swallows itself,
I think I'm done
being car parts
in a shed,
because I'm watching a bee
fuck a rosebush
and not seeing switchblades,
not counting

the number of times
I've worn anxiety
or thought my fingers
didn't belong to me,
and because I'm wearing
new shoes
and have painted my toenails
the red of balloons,
not blood transfusions,
I'm looking at a poplar tree
and understanding why owls
might couple there,
I'm feeling like a real person
with real skin, real hair,
a real heart
that isn't packed in a cooler,
real lungs tied together
not hostages,
but two people
in a bathtub,
and the spider
above my head
tunes its web
like an electric guitar,
reeling in the fly
that expected today
to go very differently,

and I'm not seeing that
as a metaphor
for my love life,
not feeling like plaque
in an artery,
a ransacked castle
with its drawbridge up,
I'm not losing my name
in someone else's cigarette
or looking into eyes
and seeing zeroes,
so I think I'm ready
to spit out
the needle-nose pliers
in my mouth,
I think I'm done
being a dimmer switch,
because it's October,
and I'm touching your face,
which feels like a face.

ACKNOWLEDGMENTS

I am incredibly grateful to the editors of the following publications in which these poems first appeared, sometimes in different forms:

"January," *CutBank Literary Magazine*

"Shadowboxing" ("To let grief ride my blood..."), "Box of Shadows," *Tupelo Quarterly*

"Hotel," *West Branch*

"Halloween," "If the Body Is a Door," *The Journal*

"Atropine," "Mountain," *Bear Review*

"Tiny Shotgun," "Cactus," *Harpur Palate*

"Bobsled," "Falling Action," *BOAAT*

"Shadowboxing" ("Here are the sex cries..."), "Nesting Dolls," "Bridge, Shadow, Hand," *Jet Fuel Review*

"Poem for Spring," *ZYZZYVA*

"Tuning Fork," *Rattle*

"One Spring," "Everyone I Love Is Drafting Their Own Eulogies," *Springhouse Journal*

"Shadowboxing" ("I was waiting for my hairpins..."), *Prairie Schooner*

"Sidewalk," *The Paris-American*

"Because It's October," *Tin House* (Broadside Thirty Series)

"January" was chosen by Matt Rasmussen for *CutBank Literary Magazine*'s Patricia Goedicke Prize in Poetry.

"Shadowboxing" ("To let grief ride my blood...") and "Box of Shadows" were chosen by Amaud Jamaul Johnson as finalists in *Tupelo Quarterly*'s TQ5 Poetry Contest.

"Shadowboxing" ("Here are the sex cries...") is after Jackson Burgess.

"Nesting Dolls" was named Editor's Pick for *Jet Fuel Review* Issue #10

"Sidewalk" was chosen by Marie Howe as a finalist in *The Paris-American*'s 2014 Reading Series Contest.

Thank you to my incredible mentors, whose poetry, wisdom, and generosity I am endlessly grateful for: Natalie Diaz, David St. John, Cecilia Woloch, and Matthew Zapruder. Thank you to Matthew Dickman for your thoughtful reading of the first draft and all of your support since. Thank you to Tin House and its Summer Writers' Workshop. Many thanks to the University of Southern California's English Department and School of Pharmacy and to Mission Road Pharmacy.

Infinite gratitude to my writer friends, who have read the many iterations of these poems and still choose to spend time with me. Thank you to all who workshopped these poems with me at Tin House, at USC, in Paris. Special thanks to Jackson Burgess, Lisa Locascio, August Lührs, Douglas Manuel, and Adam Phillips, whose feedback was instrumental in the shaping of this book.

Thank you to Marli Gitelson, my always-twin. Thank you to the Phillips and Bisno families. Much love to my wonderful friends from The Buckley School, USC, and USC's School of Pharmacy, without whom I would be a much sadder person with much sadder poems.

I am so grateful for the kindness and editorial insight of Carl Adamshick and Natalie Garyet, who made working on this book an incredible collaborative experience. Thank you to the brilliant Anya Roberts-Toney for creating the cover image.

So much love and gratitude to my parents, Dana and Michael Madievsky, who somehow convinced me that pharmacist-poet was a feasible profession. Adam Madievsky, I'm proud to be your sister. Thank you to my grandparents, my aunts, uncles and cousins, and to the rest of my wonderful family for loving and supporting me always.

Endless thanks to Adam Phillips, who inspires me constantly and whom I love dearly.

And thank you, dear reader.

TAVERN BOOKS

Tavern Books is a not-for-profit poetry publisher that exists to print, promote, and preserve works of literary vision, to foster a climate of cultural preservation, and to disseminate books in a way that benefits the reading public.

We publish books in translation from the world's finest poets, champion new works by innovative writers, and revive of out-of-print classics. We keep our titles in print, honoring the cultural contract between publisher and author, as well as between publisher and public. Our catalog, known as The Living Library, sustains the visions of our authors, ensuring their voices remain alive in the social and artistic discourse of our modern era.

ABOUT THE WROLSTAD
CONTEMPORARY POETRY SERIES

To honor the life and work of Greta Wrolstad (1981-2005), author of *Night is Simply a Shadow* (2013) and *Notes on Sea & Shore* (2010), Tavern Books invites submissions of new poetry collections through the Wrolstad Contemporary Poetry Series during an annual reading period.

This series exists to champion exceptional literary works from young women poets through a book publication in The Living Library, the Tavern Books catalog of innovative poets ranging from first-time authors and neglected masters to Pulitzer Prize winners and Nobel Laureates. The Wrolstad Contemporary Poetry Series is open to any woman aged 40 years or younger who is a US citizen, regardless of publication history.

For more information visit: tavernbooks.org/wrolstad-series

SELECTED LIVING LIBRARY TITLES

Arthur's Talk with the Eagle by Anonymous,
translated from the Welsh by Gwyneth Lewis

Ashulia by Zubair Ahmed

Breckinridge County Suite by Joe Bolton

*My People & Other Poems by Wojciech Bonowicz,
translated from the Polish by Piotr Florczyk

Buson: Haiku by Yosa Buson,
translated from the Japanese by Franz Wright

Evidence of What Is Said by Ann Charters and Charles Olson

Who Whispered Near Me by Killarney Clary

The End of Space by Albert Goldbarth

Six-Minute Poems: The Last Poems
by George Hitchcock

The Wounded Alphabet: Collected Poems
by George Hitchcock

Hitchcock on Trial
by George Hitchcock

My Blue Piano by Else Lasker-Schüler,
translated from the German by Eavan Boland

Why We Live in the Dark Ages by Megan Levad

Archeology by Adrian C. Louis

Fire Water World & Among the Dog Eaters
by Adrian C. Louis

Emergency Brake by Ruth Madievsky

Under an Arkansas Sky by Jo McDougall

The Undiscovered Room by Jo McDougall

Ocean by Joseph Millar

Petra by Amjad Nasser,
translated from the Arabic by Fady Joudah

The Fire's Journey: Part I by Eunice Odio,
translated from the Spanish by Keith Ekiss
with Sonia P. Ticas and Mauricio Espinoza

The Fire's Journey: Part II by Eunice Odio,
translated from the Spanish by Keith Ekiss
with Sonia P. Ticas and Mauricio Espinoza

*The Fire's Journey: Part III by Eunice Odio,
translated from the Spanish by Keith Ekiss
with Sonia P. Ticas and Mauricio Espinoza

*The Fire's Journey: Part IV by Eunice Odio,
translated from the Spanish by Keith Ekiss
with Sonia P. Ticas and Mauricio Espinoza

Duino Elegies by Rainer Maria Rilke,
translated from the German by Gary Miranda

Twelve Poems about Cavafy by Yannis Ritsos,
translated from the Greek by Paul Merchant

Glowing Enigmas by Nelly Sachs,
translated from the German by Michael Hamburger

Tavern Books is funded, in part, by the generosity of philanthropic organizations, public and private institutions, and individual donors. By supporting Tavern Books and its mission, you enable us to publish the most exciting poets from around the world. To learn more about underwriting Tavern Books titles, please contact us by e-mail: info@tavernbooks.org.

MAJOR FUNDING HAS BEEN PROVIDED BY

THE PUBLICATION OF THIS BOOK IS MADE POSSIBLE, IN PART, BY THE SUPPORT OF THE FOLLOWING INDIVIDUALS

Gabriel Boehmer

Dean & Karen Garyet

Mark Swartz & Jennifer Jones

The Mancini Family

Mary Ann Ryan

Marjorie Simon

Bill & Leah Stenson

Dan Wieden

Ron & Kathy Wrolstad

COLOPHON

This book was designed and typeset by Eldon Potter at Bryan Potter Design, Portland, Oregon. Text is set in Garamond, an old-style serif typeface named for the punch-cutter Claude Garamond (c. 1480-1561). Display font is a version of Bodoni, namesake of printer and typographer Giambattista Bodoni (1740–1813). *Emergency Brake* appears in both paperback and cloth-covered editions. Printed on archival-quality paper by McNaughton & Gunn, Inc.